Curious Critters of the Natural World

INSECTS & SPIDERS

Zephyr Press

Chicago

Library of Congress Cataloging-in-Publication Data
Is available from the Library of Congress

Curious Critters of the Natural World: Insects and Spiders
Grades 4–7

©2004 Zephyr Press

Printed in the United States of America

ISBN: 1-56976-158-2

Design and Production: Dan Miedaner
Illustrations: Terry Allen
Many of the photo images used herein were obtained from IMSI's Masterclips/MasterPhotos
collection, 1895 Francisco Blvd., East, San Rafael, CA 94901-5506
Other photo images and clip art have been obtained from Microsoft Clip Gallery Live and are used
under the terms of the End User License Agreement for Microsoft Front Page 2000.
Cover: Dan Miedaner

Published by:
Zephyr Press
An imprint of Chicago Review Press
814 North Franklin Street
Chicago, Illinois 60610
(800) 232-2187
www.zephyrpress.com

 Zephyr Press is a registered trademark of Chicago Review Press, Inc.

Contents

Teachers' Notes

Introduction

Curious Critters of the Natural World is a series of three activity books: Insects & Spiders, Mammals, and Reptiles & Amphibians. Each has an accompanying CD-ROM, referred to as the Alternet, and links to a content-controlled Internet website. These multimedia-based resources are designed to provide teachers of gifted children ages nine and over with informative and challenging extension activities based around a motivating theme of animals. Although designed for gifted students, the activities can provide motivating and enriching learning experiences for all students. Through using these materials, students will learn and use a range of skills, including these:

- reading and interpreting given information
- summarizing given information
- making generalizations based on given information
- using and comparing tables and charts

The primary objective of the *Curious Critters of the Natural World* series is to provide an instructional plan and accompanying resources for exceptional students who benefit from a differentiated curriculum. We have structured the activity books for students working in pullout situations, but the activities can also be used in the regular classroom. Use of the materials is not necessarily restricted to gifted students, and students can be selected to participate based on their abilities, needs, and interests. The key to this approach, which we term the appropriate curriculum model, is that students are presented with activities appropriate to their levels of understanding of the content and mastery of the requisite higher-order thinking processes.

Background

With gifted students, the teacher's main role is to ensure that the appropriate conditions for learning are present (Parke 1992). Doing so means helping students to learn the skills necessary to use a differentiated curriculum that provides advanced content and requires higher-order thinking processes. Moreover, Sandra

Berger (1991) describes how to tailor the learning process and environment for gifted students.

Such students benefit from

- curriculum content that is thematic, broad based, and integrative
- learning processes that encourage the use of higher-order skills through open-ended activities
- a receptive and nonjudgmental learning environment that promotes self-directed learning
- learning products that require students to evaluate real-world problems and synthesize information rather than simply summarize facts.

Certain activity pages concentrate on extending students' creative-thinking abilities. These activities are based on Edward de Bono's assertion that creativity is a skill that can be learned and improved with practice (see, for example, De Bono 1986a, b). On these pages, you will find a list of basic thinking skills that can be taught to children of all ages, and their application to problem-solving situations related to the topic under study.

The Appropriate Curriculum Model

In this book, we provide materials at three different content levels, which are adapted from Bloom's (1984) taxonomy. The table on page 3 shows for each level the code that identifies it (look for the code at the top of each activity page), the level of thinking tapped, and the types of activities students engage in.

Moving through the Content Levels

Higher-order activities have to be founded on a solid base of knowledge, which level 1 and 2 activities are designed to establish and expand. Never assume that any student has the requisite content knowledge, but be prepared to advance students quickly to higher-level activities if they demonstrate understanding of the facts and concepts presented in levels 1 and 2. As a rule of thumb, gifted students would complete minimal level 1 activities to confirm their knowledge base, do some application activities at level 2 to consolidate their knowledge, then concentrate on higher-order activities at level 3 to extend and challenge their thinking. In contrast, typical students would spend extensive time on level 1 activities, to establish a strong knowledge base, before moving on to level 2. They would remain at level 2 until they are proficient in applying their knowledge, leaving relatively less time for these students to work on the higher-order skills in level 3. Rely on your best professional judgment and information from classroom and other tests in deciding which activities, at which levels, to present to particular students.

Content Level	Code	Thinking Processes Targeted	Sample Student Activities
1	*	**Finding out:** Recalling data; showing understanding through restating or extending ideas	Answering factual questions, interpreting information, or describing or illustrating events through writing, listing, drawing, and the like
2	**	**Using information:** Applying basic knowledge to make interpretations or analyze new situations	Using knowledge for problem-solving tasks such as comparing, investigating, classifying, or generating solutions
3	***	**Creating and evaluating:** Applying and combining the content base learned in levels 1 and 2 to develop new products or concepts and make judgments	Using their extended knowledge base to invent, plan, construct, imagine, improve on, make selections, defend points of view, evaluate, or make recommendations

Components

By combining traditional information sources, such as reference books and written materials, with the enormous information capabilities of the Internet and the appeal of a computer database on the Alternet CD-ROM, *Curious Critters of the Natural World* offers teachers a three-pronged approach to student education. Because activities at the various levels use different methods of information retrieval, not all students will need to use a computer or Internet hookup at the same time, easing the pressure on available computer facilities. For each topic in the series there is an activity book, Alternet CD-ROM, and links to an Internet website, as described in the following sections. Those activities labeled "research" in the table of contents require students to use print (or software-based) reference sources in addition to the Curious Critters materials. It is wise to review these in advance in order to select and gather appropriate reference materials for your students.

Activity Book

The activity book contains worksheets at the three content levels of the appropriate curriculum model described previously. The materials are designed to be used flexibly, depending on your available computer hardware and the needs of your students. To enable you to prepare lessons without accessing the Alternet CD-ROM, its contents are reproduced in appendices at the back of this book. These pages are also handy for students who may not have computer access (for example, if activities are assigned as homework).

Most sections in the activity book can stand alone, in that students do not have to complete particular activities at an earlier level in order to work successfully on higher-level activities. This organization is based on a philosophy that gifted students should not be required to work through a sequential series of activities if they have already demonstrated a sufficient knowledge base to move directly to level 2 or 3 activities. On the other hand, it is important to confirm that students do have the requisite background knowledge, rather than automatically assuming that students labeled "gifted" are ready to move directly to higher-order activities and that those who are not so labeled are not. In addition, many of the activities at level 3 have no one correct answer. This may be threatening to students who are used to always knowing the right answer, so it is important to talk with and prepare students for this new paradigm of learning.

Alternet CD-ROM

The CD-ROM contains a database of HTML files containing information and images related to the topic of study (that is, insects and spiders, mammals, or reptiles and amphibians). Called the Alternet, it simulates the World Wide Web and is navigated in exactly the same way, through browsers. Thus, students can practice Internet-style research in a setting that controls the content and level of difficulty of the material. Activity pages labeled "Alternet" on the table of contents, and marked with the ALTERNET logo, direct students to gather specific information from the CD-ROM to complete the worksheet. Most of the level 1 Alternet activity pages require basic data gathering and are based almost entirely on information contained on the CD-ROM, allowing students to complete them without access to other reference materials. The Alternet is used less frequently in levels 2 and 3, sometimes in conjunction with other reference materials.

Internet Activities

Activity pages showing the INTERNET logo lend a contemporary and exciting aspect to learning. Most of these Internet-based activities are open-ended tasks at level 3. The materials assume that students have some understanding of how to navigate the World Wide Web and open various Internet addresses, so it is helpful to give students a basic orientation to the Internet before having them attempt these activities independently.

All the sites students are directed to have been screened for age-appropriate and relevant content. Links to all the sites are contained on the Ready Ed Publications website, which can be reached by going to **www.readyed.com.au/urls/critters.** (Bookmark this site for easy access later.) Accessing other Internet sites through the Ready Ed Publications site has several advantages over having students type in the URLs printed on the worksheet pages: The site provides direct links to specific websites, so students do not have to type in (and possibly mistype) lengthy URLs. In addition, the site is monitored regularly and links updated as the Internet evolves, to ensure students successfully reach the correct location.

From the home page, simply select the name of the activity book (e.g., "Insects & Spiders") to reach the appropriate book index, then click on the page number and title corresponding to the worksheet being completed. The student then reaches a text introduction and relevant links to begin the tasks on the page.

Hardware Requirements

To use either the Alternet or Internet activities, you will need a computer containing a frames-capable browser, either Microsoft Internet Explorer or Netscape Navigator. The CD-ROM is compatible with both Macintosh and Windows operating systems. The CD-ROM automatically opens HTML files in the Explorer or Navigator browser without accessing the Internet, so an Internet hookup is not required to use it.

System Requirements

Windows:
- Microsoft Windows 95 or higher
- 56 Color SVGA monitor
- At least Netscape 4 or Microsoft Internet Explorer 4
- 7 MB of hard drive space
- CD-ROM drive

Macintosh:
- Net-capable browser
- 7 MB of hard drive space
- At least System 7
- CD-ROM drive

Preparation for Starting a Unit

❏ Determine how best to use these materials with your students:
- As teacher-directed lessons with an individual student or group: You select which worksheets students are to complete, provide supplementary instruction as appropriate, and record the students' progress.
- As student-directed lessons: Children work through the materials at their own pace during specified periods and record their own progress.
- As an interest-based approach: Students choose the materials they want to work on and complete them during free or independent learning time. They monitor the work they complete and record their own progress.

- As supplementary materials to a unit of study: Use Curious Critters to enrich your regular curriculum by providing teacher-directed, student-directed, or interest-based lessons as appropriate.

❑ Plan lessons around these materials. Here are questions to consider:
  - What end product (or choice of end products) will students produce to show their learning (a booklet, a display, etc.)?
  - How will students work on the contents (usually either individually or in small groups)?
  - How will students access supplemental reference sources? Will you provide a selection, or will they be responsible for finding their own materials in the library?
  - What people or organizations might supplement the Curious Critters lessons (e.g., as guest speakers or field trip destinations)?
  - How will you implement the lessons in the classroom (e.g., scheduling computer time, distribution of materials, provision of art materials and supplies, procedures for grading)?

❑ Assemble a collection of appropriate reference books or materials for the unit you are working on. Or perhaps generate a bibliography to guide students in finding appropriate reference materials in the school library.

❑ For Alternet lessons, load the CD-ROM. For faster operation, make a folder labeled "Curious Critters" on your hard drive. Copy the contents of the CD-ROM to that folder, then remove the CD-ROM and store it in a safe location. To access the files directly from the CD-ROM, follow these steps; to access files copied on to your hard drive, begin with step 4:

1. Insert the CD-ROM.
2. Click on "My Computer" (Windows Desktop), or open the folder in the usual way for Macintosh computers.
3. Click on the CD-ROM drive.
4. Click on the folder "Curious Critters" then the file "start.htm" to display the welcome screen.
5. Click on the book you are using (e.g., "Insects & Spiders") then select the section you are working on (e.g., "Spiders.")
6. From there the instructions at the top of each activity page will tell students which sections to click on.

Note: While the Alternet program is loading, you may see warning messages about connection difficulties. These messages appear because you are using an Internet browser while not connected to the Internet. Simply click "OK" and ignore the messages.

Now you're ready to take your students on an amazing journey into the animal kingdom. We guarantee they'll be challenged and motivated to discover and explore.

References

Berger, Sandra L. 1991. *Differentiating Curriculum for Gifted Students.* ERIC Digest #E510 (ERIC Document Reproduction Service No. ED342175)

Bloom, Benjamin J. 1984. *Taxonomy of Educational Objectives: The Classification of Educational Goals.* New York: Longman.

DeBono, Edward. 1986a. The Practical Teaching of Thinking Using the CoRT Method. *Special Services in the Schools,* 3 (1–2): 33–47.

———. 1986b. A Technique for Teaching Creative Thinking. *Momentum* 17 (3): 17–19.

Parke, Beverly N. 1992. *Challenging Gifted Students in the Regular Classroom.* ERIC Digest #E513 (ERIC Document Reproduction Service No. ED352774)

❋ **Level 1 Activities**

Finding Out about Insects—1
(Go to the Alternet CD-ROM section: What is an Insect?)

Anatomy

1. The information on the CD-ROM describes an insect as "any living _____
_____ ."

2. Name the three regions of an insect's body. Use the links to describe each.

    a. _____   _____

    _____   _____

    b. _____   _____

    _____   _____

    c. _____   _____

    _____   _____

3. Use the diagrams on the Alternet CD-ROM to help complete this picture. Draw and/or label these body parts: antenna, simple and compound eye, mouth, ear, wing, spiracles, ovipositor, legs. Use lines to segment off the three regions of the body. Label them.

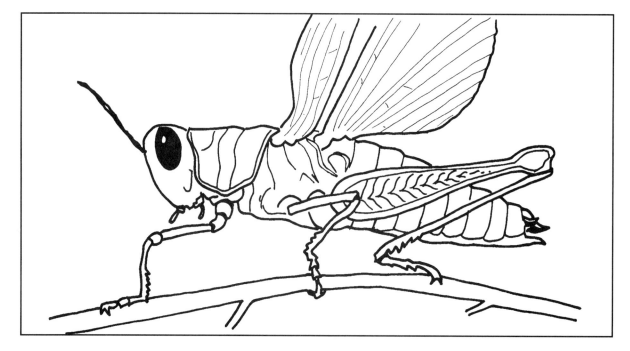

4. Use the links on the Alternet CD-ROM to define these insect features:

    exoskeleton _____

    antennae _____

    mouth parts _____

    eyes _____

Curious Critters: Insects & Spiders, © 2004 Zephyr Press, Chicago, IL • 800-232-2187 • www.zephyrpress.com

Name: _____

✽ **Level 1 Activities**

Finding Out about Insects—2
(Go to the Alternet CD-ROM section: What is an Insect?)

❑ On the CD-ROM look at the link for "range of insect species".

1. Write two key points about each of these:

a. Size _____
_____

b. Color _____
_____

c. Shape _____
_____

d. Thorax _____
_____

c. Wings _____
_____

2. Like you, insects grow and develop. However the process, called metamorphosis, shows extreme physical changes rather than our gradual changes.

a. Explain the term 'metamorphosis' by checking the link on the CD-ROM.

b. Look under the heading "The Insect Life Cycle" to describe what happens at each life stage of an insect. Write about each and draw pictures in the boxes to show what the stage looks like. Use an insect that you know about (e.g. butterfly) for your examples.

Egg _____
_____
_____

Larva _____
_____
_____

Pupa _____
_____
_____

Adult _____
_____
_____

❄ **Level 1 Activities**

Classification of Insects—1

(Go to the Alternet CD-ROM section: Classification of Insects)

There are millions of types of plants and animals which have been carefully classified into different species based on their physical characteristics. This system of classification helps scientists all over the world in their studies so they can be sure they are talking about the same species.

❏ Use the information on the CD-ROM to write some key points about each of the seven sections of the scientific classification system:

Kingdom 1. _____

2. _____

Phylum 1. _____

2. _____

Class 1. _____

2. _____

Order 1. _____

2. _____

Family _____

Genus 1. _____

2. _____

Species 1. _____

2. _____

❏ Use the table on the CD-ROM to help you complete this classification table:

	Human Beings	Madagascar Hissing Cockroach	Orangutan
Kingdom		Animalia	
	Chordata		Chordata
Class			Mammals
	Primates	Blattodea	
Family		Blattidea	
	Homo		Pongo
Species			Pygmaeus

Curious Critters: Insects & Spiders, © 2004 Zephyr Press, Chicago, IL • 800-232-2187 • www.zephyrpress.com

Name: _____

✳ **Level 1 Activities**

Classification of Insects—2
(Go to the Alternet CD-ROM section: Classification of Insects)

The classification system is a way of classifying all living things according to their physical characteristics.

❑ Use the information on the Alternet CD-ROM to answer these questions:

1. What is the largest unit of classification? _____

2. What is the basic unit of the system? _____

3. What is the scientific name for human beings? _____

4. What is the scientific name for the Madagascar hissing cockroach? _____

5. Which kingdom do insects belong to? _____

6. Which phyla do they belong to? _____

7. Which class do they belong to? _____

8. How many orders are there in the Insecta class? _____

9. What are the three different name endings for the orders and what do they mean?

   _____   _____   _____

10. Insects belong to the Arthropods group. What does the word "Arthropods" mean?

    _____

    _____

11. Name some other animals that are included in this group. _____

    _____

❑ Refer to the table at the end of the "Classification" section. What are the common names for each of these insect orders?

Phtirapetera _____

Coleoptera _____

Lepidoptera _____

Phasmatodea _____

Odanata _____

Isopters _____

Mantodea _____

❑ Draw lines to show the three parts of this insect.

SUMMARY FACT BOX

Complete these facts about insects.

All insects have these three characteristics:

1. _____

   _____

2. _____

   _____

3. _____

   _____

Complete:

The study of insects is known as:

_____

The exoskeleton is: _____

❋ ❋ Level 2 Activities

Comparing and Classifying Insects

(Reference: Alternet Introductory Section; Your Level 1 work)

Comparing

❏ In the space below construct a table showing how humans and insects can be compared according to the headings given. A start has been made for you.

	Humans	**Insects**
Shape/Form	*Essentially, all the same form and basic shape.*	
	Shape can vary between individuals.	
Growth & Development		
Skeleton		
Senses		
Eyes		
Vertebra		

Classifying

❏ Remember the criteria for an insect? Apply your knowledge by classifying these animals:

earthworm	bee	dragonfly	housefly	ladybug
louse	silverfish	scorpion	leech	spider
stinkbug	cricket	stick insect	shrimp	hornet
ant	aphid	slug	mosquito	crab
hoverfly	snail	beetle	millipede	cockroach
centipede	bedbug	dust mite	damselfly	butterfly

Insect	**Not an Insect**

Curious Critters: Insects & Spiders, © 2004 Zephyr Press, Chicago, IL • 800-232-2187 • www.zephyrpress.com

Name: _____

Insect Analysis

(For this activity you will need an insect and a magnifying glass or specimen jar with a magnified top.)

❏ Place your insect on white paper to provide a clear view. Examine it with your magnifier. Draw these parts of the insect.

The Head	The Abdomen
The Thorax	**The Antennae**

❏ Use your knowledge of insects and classification to complete the following information about the insect you are analyzing.

Classification: _____

Description: _____

Size: _____

Color: _____

Shape: _____

Wings: _____

Camouflage: _____

Adaptations: _____

Location: (Where found; where it usually lives.) _____

Dynamics: (What does it do?) _____

_____

Special features: _____

_____

Name: _____

✳ ✳ Level 2 Activities

Insects Puzzle

❑ Complete this crossword to show your understanding of insects and their lives.

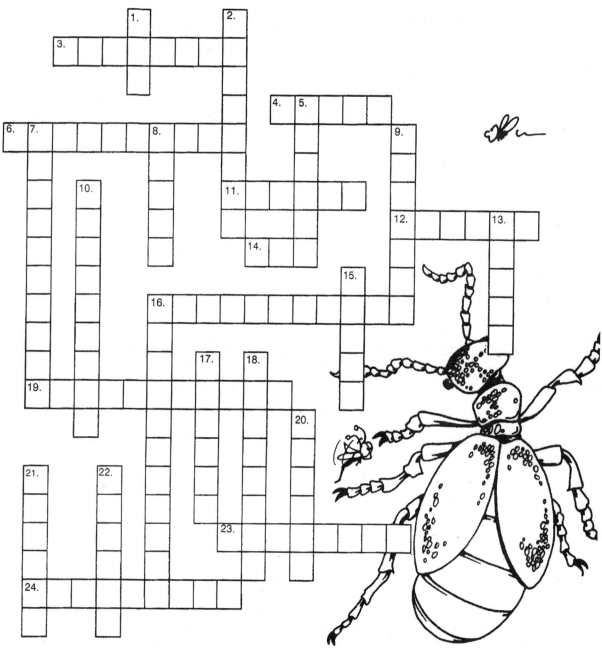

Across

3. fragile
4. poison
6. protection by coloring
11. middle part of an insect
12. a large group of ants
14. an insect that collects nectar and pollen
16. insects that eat other insects
19. outer skin
23. feelers
24. comes out at night

Down

1. number of legs on an insect
2. parts or sections
5. to come out
7. what an insect looks like
8. next stage after the "egg"
9. type or kind
10. sound movement
13. baby insect that looks like its adult
15. when a caterpillar sheds its skin
16. this becomes a butterfly

17. sweet part of a flower
18. large eyes made of tiny eyes
20. male ants
21. protect oneself
22. a hole

Curious Critters: Insects & Spiders, © 2004 Zephyr Press, Chicago, IL • 800-232-2187 • www.zephyrpress.com

Name: _____

Making Judgments—1

(This activity is an extension of the 'Insect Analysis' activity, p. 13)

❑ Make some observations and judgments on how well equipped for survival the insect you have been studying is in its natural environment.

1.a. Describe the habitat in which you found the insect. _____

_____

1.b. In what ways is the insect suited to this habitat? _____

_____

2.a. Describe how the insect moves (use of body parts, speed, direction, recognition of obstacles).

_____

_____

2.b. How does the insect's movement suit its environment? _____

_____

3.a. How 'social' does the insect appear to be? (Does it live alone, in groups?) _____

_____

3.b. What evidence is there that it is part of a community? _____

_____

❑ Try these experiments and make some judgements about the insect's living patterns.

1. What does the insect like to eat? Place a variety of foods on paper and place the insect on the edge. Observe what it does. _____

_____

_____

2. What does the insect do if touched? _____

_____

3. Place the insect in sunlight. Observe and record what it does. _____

_____

4. Place the insect in a dark place, such as a shoe box. Observe what it does. _____

_____

5. Place the insect in a box in half shade and half sun. Observe what it does. _____

_____

❑ What interpretations can you make from these observations?

_____

_____

Name: _____

Making Judgments—2
Helpful or Harmful?

❑ Over thousands of years human beings have encountered both helpful and harmful aspects of insects, with the first far outweighing the second. Use the headings to make some judgments about whether insects are helpful or harmful for the idea or people shown. Key words are given as clues. One has been done for you. Check off whether the insect action is helpful or harmful in each case.

Pollination: Bees

Many plants depend on insects such as bees to have their seeds spread in the pollination process.

☑ Helpful ❑ Harmful

Householders: Termites

❑ Helpful ❑ Harmful

Health: Disease

❑ Helpful ❑ Harmful

Environment: Soil Aerating

❑ Helpful ❑ Harmful

Farmers: Pests

❑ Helpful ❑ Harmful

Products: Silk

❑ Helpful ❑ Harmful

**Food Chain:
Food for Other Animals**

❑ Helpful ❑ Harmful

Predators: Parasites

❑ Helpful ❑ Harmful

 Curious Critters: Insects & Spiders, © 2004 Zephyr Press, Chicago, IL • 800-232-2187 • www.zephyrpress.com

Name: _____

Design and Create an Insect—1

Design Brief

❑ To show your understanding of the characteristics of insects, design an imaginary insect which might live somewhere in the world. It must have all the characteristics of a real insect but should have some unique adaptations to help it survive in its habitat. You will be building a model of your final design.

Note: Make sure you have investigated and are aware of all the characteristics of an insect.

Brainstorm

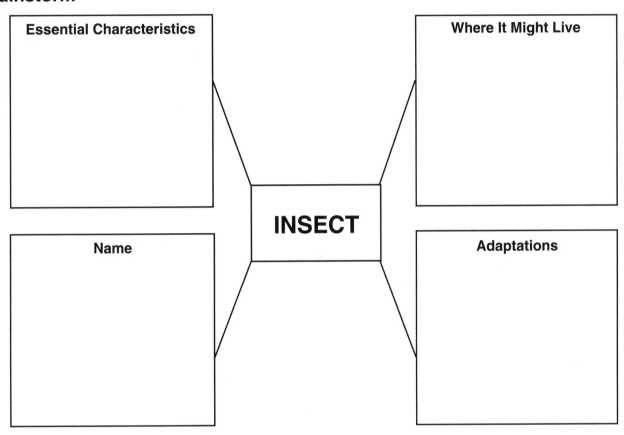

| Essential Characteristics | Where It Might Live |

INSECT

| Name | Adaptations |

Design

❑ Sketch a few ideas for your insect before deciding on one to do in detail. (Use the back of this page.) When you have chosen one insect design to develop, draw it in detail below. Your design needs to be clear so that you can build a model from it, and it should include <u>labels</u> showing what materials you need for each part.

Name: ______________________________

✻ ✻ ✻ Level 3 Activities

Design and Create an Insect—2

Creating the Insect

❑ Now comes the fun part! Use your design plans and materials to build your insect. If you need to change any part of your original design, draw your modifications and say why you changed from your original design. Option: You may like to create an environment (setting) for your insect.

Evaluation

1. Did your insect include all the characteristics of a real insect? (List the characteristics and check each one.)

____

____

2. Did you use your original design? ______________________________

3. If you modified your design, did you include the changes, details and reasons why you changed?

____

4. Are you happy with your insect's appearance? ______________________

5. Are you happy with the materials you selected? ______________________

6. What changes would you make if you did this design again? ______________

____

____

Scientific Report

❑ Write a scientific report giving all the important information on your imaginary insect.

Insect Name: ______________________________

Classification: (What is it? Family name?) ______________________

____

Description: (What attributes does it have, e.g. size, shape, features?) ____________

____

____

Location: (Where is it found?) ______________________

____

Dynamics: (What does it do?) ______________________

____

Summarizing Comment: ______________________

____

____

____

Curious Critters: Insects & Spiders, © 2004 Zephyr Press, Chicago, IL • 800-232-2187 • www.zephyrpress.com

✳ ✳ ✳ **Level 3 Activities**

Insects Internet Tasks

(Website: Click on Curious Critters: Insects and Spiders, Page 19 and Site 1, 2 or 3 .)

❑ Use the Internet sites to complete one or more of the tasks detailed below:

Site 1: Introduction to Insects and Site 2: Wonderful World of Insects

This site contains information on all aspects of insects. Choose one of the insects that interests you and create a display about it. Avoid simply copying out a whole lot of notes! Use pictures, models, anatomy diagrams, dioramas, posters, comic strips and/or any other display features you can think of. Make sure you consider questions such as:

- Is there a better alternative for the controlling of insect pests, rather than simply killing them?

- What if bees (or your insect) totally disappeared? What would be the consequences for us and the living world?

Site 2: Antboys Bugworld

- Refer to this site and the links for ants, bees, roaches and other bugs.

- Read the information, concentrating on the social aspect of how these insects live.

- Use your understanding to create a booklet on social insects. Concentrate on how they socialize in order to live. Compare this social aspect to that of humans. How are we the same? How are we different?

Site 3: Bee Eye

- This site presents an idea of what objects look like through the eye of a bee.

- Use the information and activities to find out about compound eyes and their relationship to simple eyes. Use your findings to help you construct a series of diagrams on what a chair, a flower or a person would look like to a bee.

- Extend your diagrams to a painting showing the patterns that might appear to a bee as it uses its compound eyes.

Name: _____

Insects: Creative-Thinking Task Sheet

❏ An increased understanding of the skills shown below will help to develop your ability to think more creatively. What to do: Apply the skill to the Insects theme by following the instructions. Work on a large sheet of paper to end up with a chain of ideas, something like this:

Fluency The idea here is to come up with as many ideas as possible in the set time.	List all the insects you can think of in a two-minute time period.
Flexibility Try to provide as big a variety of ideas as you can.	Compare a bee with an ant. List the ways they are: • alike • different
Originality Provide new or unique solutions; perhaps put two known ideas together to form a third.	Compose a limerick (5-line poem—Lines 1, 2 & 5 rhyme; Lines 3 & 4 rhyme) about an insect that interests you.
Elaboration Add on to what you already know to make an idea more exciting.	Improve an ant so that it can help you with your homework. What do you need to do? What ant features can you maintain or improve on?
Curiosity Seek answers to questions by using Who? What? How? Why?	What would happen if bees disappeared from the earth?
Complexity Look for different alternatives to what is provided or what you already know.	What questions can be asked to find out why a ladybug has bright colors? Write five.
Risk taking Accepting that there may be more than one correct answer but if you are mistaken that it doesn't equal failure.	Rank these insects according to three different aspects—butterflies, bees, ants. Say what your rankings are based on. Say why you ranked them as you did in each case.
Imagination Think beyond what is usually accepted as correct or true.	Pretend that cockroaches have overruled the world. Why? What would happen?

Curious Critters: Insects & Spiders, © 2004 Zephyr Press, Chicago, IL • 800-232-2187 • www.zephyrpress.com

✳ **Level 1 Activities**

Butterflies and Moths—1
(Go to the Alternet CD-ROM section: Butterflies and Moths)

❏ Use the picture on the CD-ROM to complete this diagram. Label important body parts.

1. Write some key points about each of these:

a. Head—The four main parts are:

1. _____

2. _____

3. _____

4. _____

b. Abdomen—contains _____ parts.

These include: _____

_____

c. Thorax—contains _____ parts.

These parts contain: _____

and: _____

2. Describe the physical features of the different stages by filling in the table below:

STAGE:	Caterpillar (larval stage)
Color	
Skin	
Body segments	
Spinneret	
	Pupa
Exoskeleton (What happens to the exoskeleton?)	
Describe the transformation that occurs.	
	Adult
Exoskeleton (What happens at this stage?)	
Proboscis	

Name: _____

❋ ❋ **Level 2 Activities**

Butterflies and Moths—2

(Go to the Alternet CD-ROM section: Butterflies and Moths)

❑ Quiz. Use the information on the CD-ROM to answer these questions:

1. How many segments is a butterfly caterpillar made up of? _____

2. Which segment of the caterpillar contains the head? _____

3. Name the organ that allows the caterpillar to spin a thread. _____

4. How long does the caterpillar stage usually last? _____

5. What does the newly emerged butterfly use to join the split proboscis?

6. After about how long does it take for the butterfly to be ready to fly following its emergence from the pupa stage? _____

7. What do moths spin to protect the pupa? _____

8. The life span of a butterfly varies from _____ to _____

❑ Use the information on the CD-ROM to complete this Comparison Chart.

Comparison Chart: Butterflies and Moths

■ Look at the CD-ROM to find out how moths are different from butterflies. Write the differences in the appropriate column.

Butterflies	**Moths**
_____	_____
_____	_____
_____	_____
_____	_____

■ What features do butterflies and moths have in common with all other insects? Name them.

_____

_____

_____

_____

■ Draw a caterpillar.

Curious Critters: Insects & Spiders, © 2004 Zephyr Press, Chicago, IL • 800-232-2187 • www.zephyrpress.com

Name: _____

✿ ✿ ✿ **Level 3 Activities**

Butterflies and Moths—3

(Website: Click on Curious Critters: Butterflies and Moths, Page 23 and Site 1.)

Create-a-Book

The website that the link above takes you to will allow you to gather the information and graphics necessary to complete the task below.

❑ Your Task: Use the Internet site to help you create a book for young readers on "The Life Cycle of a Butterfly." Use the art work provided at the site as the basis for each page. Follow the instructions to print out each picture. Use the notes as the basis for the text you are putting in the book. However, reword it as it is probably too difficult for the young readers your book is aimed at. Perhaps you could make the topic more appealing by building a story of a fictional butterfly, basing it on the factual elements detailed on the website.

A page from your book might look like this example:

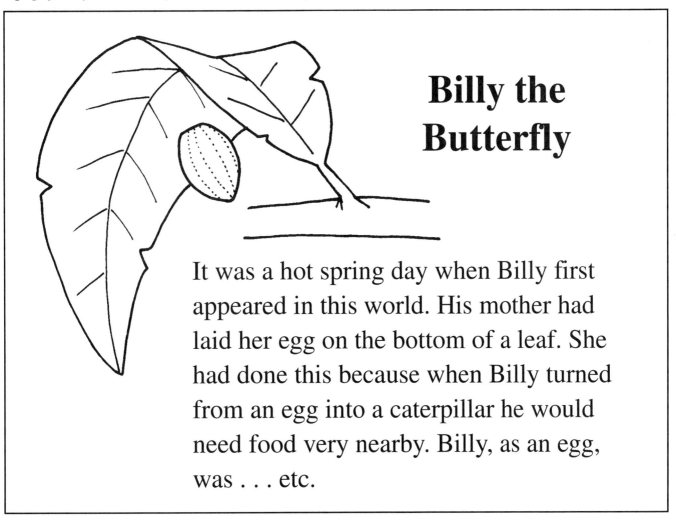

Billy the Butterfly

It was a hot spring day when Billy first appeared in this world. His mother had laid her egg on the bottom of a leaf. She had done this because when Billy turned from an egg into a caterpillar he would need food very nearby. Billy, as an egg, was . . . etc.

Name: _____

✳ / ✳ ✳ Level 1/2 Activities

Social Insects: The Honeybee

(Go to the Alternet CD-ROM section: Social Insects—The Honeybee Colony)

❑ Honeybees are the best known of the social bees. They live, share food, and work with tens of thousands of family members in one large bee colony. Use the CD-ROM to help you learn all about these amazing insects. Complete the questions below. What three kinds of bees are found in a honeybee colony? Fill in the table below to show the physical features and behavior for each type.

Name:			
Physical characteristics			
Special features			
Behavior			
Role in the colony What jobs do they do?			

❑ Use the CD-ROM to provide information on these points:

- The beehive: _____
  _____
  _____

- How a bee uses its sting: _____
  _____
  _____

- How honey is produced: _____
  _____
  _____

- What swarming is: _____
  _____
  _____

Name: _____

First go to www.readyed.com.au/urls/critters

✽ ✽ ✽ **Level 3 Activities**

Social Insects: Working Together

(Website: Click on Curious Critters: Social Insects, Page 25, Site 1, 2 & 3.)

❑ Social insects are characterized by the ways in which they function together as a colony. In what ways are insects such as honeybees and ants judged to be 'social'? Visit the websites shown and make some judgements on how this 'social' aspect can be applied to the words underlined below. Then, complete a report on Social Insects, emphasizing your conclusions about what makes some insects 'social'.

- Look for information on how the <u>habitat</u> shows the insects' social nature.

- Look for information on how the various <u>roles</u> undertaken within the colony show the social nature of the insects.

- Look for information on how <u>mating habits</u> show the insects' social nature.

- Look for information on how <u>food collection</u> shows the social nature of the insects.

❑ Make your initial notes here:

**Ants
(Site 1)**

**Honeybees
(Sites 2, 3)**

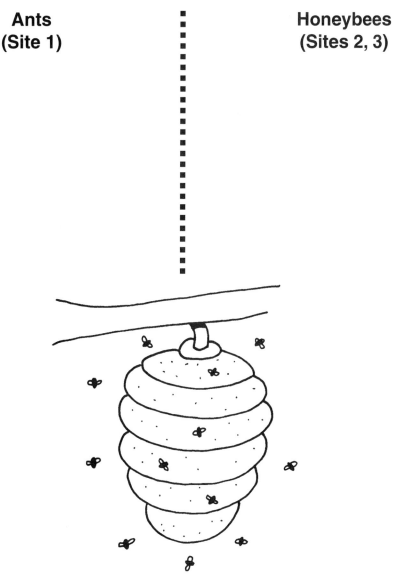

✳ **Level 1 Activities**

Common Insects: Beetles

(Go to the Alternet CD-ROM section: Common Insects—Types of Beetles)

Beetles, although possessing the same characteristics as many other insect types, come in a fantastic range of shapes, sizes and colors. Read about some of the different beetle families on the CD-ROM and then complete the activities below.

Beetle Families

❏ Name and describe these beetle families. Fill in the table below using information from the Alternet. Draw or paste a picture into the space for each type of beetle.

Beetle Family	Number of Species	Identifying Features	Diet	Picture
Weevils				
Ground Beetles				
Ladybugs				
Fireflies				
Rove Beetles				
Scarabs				
Click Beetles				
Predacious Diving Beetles				

Name: _____

Use the CD-ROM with this page.

Common Insects: Flies
(Go to the Alternet CD-ROM section: Common Insects—Fearless Flies)

A Fly's Life

❑ Flies are one of the most common insects and definitely one of the most annoying. There are many different types of flies and most are capable of spreading deadly diseases. Use the Alternet CD-ROM to learn more about these insects and complete the activities below. Describe and draw the four stages involved in the life cycle of the fly.

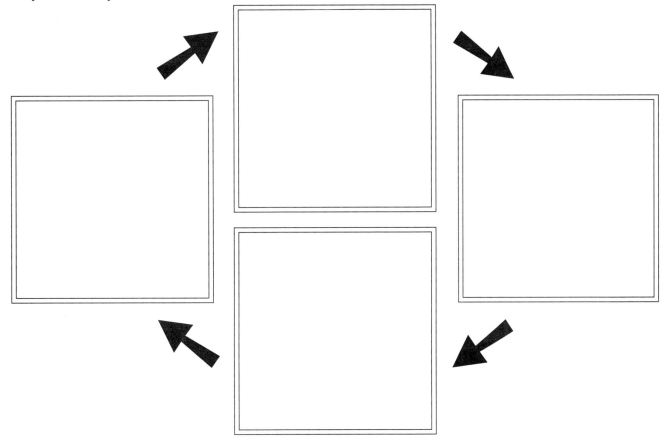

❑ Use the CD-ROM to help you make some FACT CARDS about these insect types. Write three key points about each insect.

Fruit Fly	Mosquito	Sand Fly	Tsetse Fly

Name: _____

Common Insects: The Ladybug Report

❑ Rewrite the "Random Facts" below under these report headings: Classification, Description, Location, Dynamics (Movements and Actions), Special Features.

❑ Use your notes to write a full report on the ladybug.

Random Facts

1. Has a strong thickened head and thorax.

2. Exposure to air hardens the ladybug's shell.

3. Adult can eat 60 aphids a day.

4. Mouthparts adapted for chewing and grinding.

5. Hibernates during winter, under leaves or loose bark.

6. Has six legs.

7. Red or yellow with black, red, white or yellow spots. Some have stripes.

8. Also called a ladybird (U.K.).

9. Defends itself by pulling in its legs and playing dead.

10. Round body, shaped like half a pea.

11. Has hard, upper pair of wings, thickened into shields.

12. Part of species of beetles.

13. Has second pair of flying wings tucked under outer hard wings.

14. Ladybugs help plants by eating plant-eating insects.

15. Scientific name—Coleoptera.

16. Newly emerged ladybug has a soft, opaque shell.

17. Ladybug larva can eat 500 aphids a day.

18. Built like armored tanks.

19. Enemies of ladybugs are birds, spiders, ants and toads.

20. Helpful to fruit growers.

21. Can gather in large groups to hibernate.

22. When threatened it squeezes out a foul-smelling liquid from its legs.

23. Part of the largest order of animals in the world.

24. Feeds chiefly on aphids and scale insects.

25. Ladybugs are said to bring good luck.

26. Lives in forests, fields, parks and gardens.

Name: _____

Common Insects: Classifying

❏ Scientifically, insects are classified into specific categories so that we can make comparisons and tell the differences between species. However, we can also classify insects according to other criteria. Use your understanding of common insects to provide some information under the following classifications:

1. Insects that can be classified as pests to humans:

Name   What makes it a pest?

1. _____   _____

2. _____   _____

3. _____   _____

2. Insects that can be classified as dangerous to humans:

Name   What makes it dangerous?

1. _____   _____

2. _____   _____

3. _____   _____

3. Insects that can be classified as helpful to humans:

Name   What makes it helpful?

1. _____   _____

2. _____   _____

3. _____   _____

❏ Draw one of the insects you've listed above and label it as a pest, dangerous or helpful.

✳ ✳ ✳ **Level 3 Activities**

Common Insects: Brilliant Beetles

(Website: Click on Curious Critters: Common Insects, Page 30, Site 1.)

❏ This website makes the statement that, when compared with all living creatures, "beetles might be the most successful creatures on earth." Use the website to find 10 statements to support this argument:

1. *(e.g. The life cycle of beetles involves the complete metamorphosis cycle of egg, larva, pupa and adult.* _____
   For protection some beetle types keep their eggs inside their bodies and give birth to live larvae.) _____

2. _____
   _____

3. _____
   _____

4. _____
   _____

5. _____
   _____

6. _____
   _____

7. _____
   _____

8. _____
   _____

9. _____
   _____

10. _____
    _____

❏ Do you agree with the statement about beetles made at the top of this page?
On what do you base your judgement?

_____
_____
_____
_____

Curious Critters: Insects & Spiders, © 2004 Zephyr Press, Chicago, IL • 800-232-2187 • www.zephyrpress.com

Name: ____________________

Use the CD-ROM with this page.

❋ **Level 1 Activities**

Beneficial Insects: Praying Mantis—1

(Go to the Alternet CD-ROM section: Beneficial Insects—Praying Mantis)

The praying mantis is an unusual insect that is considered to be of great benefit to humans rather than a pest, as it preys on many other insect pests. Read about the unique habits of mantids on the CD-ROM and complete the activities below.

Habitat

❑ Describe the areas and locations that the praying mantis is found in. ____________________

____

Classification

❑ Complete the following.

The praying mantis gets its name from a Greek word meaning ____________________ .

It belongs to the sub-order ____________________ which is one of the orders of the class ____________________. Sometimes this mantid is referred to as a ____________________mantis because of its preying on other insects and small creatures.

❑ Search the CD links to find information on the following features of the praying mantis.

Forelegs: ____________________

____

Camouflage: ____________________

____

Echolocation: ____________________

____

Startle display: ____________________

____

Ultrasonic ear: ____________________

____

What the Insect Looks Like

❑ Use the photos on the CD to help you draw a diagram of a praying mantis. Label these parts: head, abdomen, thorax, wings, forelegs, antennae, ear

Name: _____

Beneficial Insects: Praying Mantis—2

❏ Scattered below are 'random facts' about the praying mantis. Sort the 'random facts information under the headings in the chart. Use the information you collect to write a paragraph for each section and create a report on the praying mantis.

Hatches from eggs

Male smaller than female

Green or brown coloring

2 pairs of fine wings

Can stay very still for hours on end

1800 species

Catches prey with spiny forelegs

Long sharp claws

Strong jaws

Scientific name—Mantis Religiosa

Some nymphs eat each other

Eaten by birds

Has good camouflage

Has a flexible neck

Has a triangular head

Looks like a leaf or a twig

Lives in trees and grassland

Size 1.5–2.75 inches (4–7 cm) long

Gets its name by sitting on its hind legs, while neatly folding its forelegs in front

Doesn't have good defences other than camouflage

Long, slender body

Eggs hatch into nymphs

Eats other insects and spiders

Has powerful jaws

Three pairs of legs

Found in tropical and warm countries

Eggs laid in large cocoon

Female lays 200–400 eggs at a time

Large compound eyes

Can see behind without turning its head—has all round vision

Classification:

Description:

Location:

Dynamics:

Special Features:

Curious Critters: Insects & Spiders, © 2004 Zephyr Press, Chicago, IL • 800-232-2187 • www.zephyrpress.com

First go to www.readyed.com.au/urls/critters

✽ ✽ **Level 2 Activities**

Beneficial Insects: Silkworms

(Website: Click on Curious Critters: Beneficial Insects, Page 33, Site 1.)

❏ 'Silk worm' is the common name for the silk producing larvae from a number of different species of moth such as the *Bombyx mori*, the domesticated silkworm moth. These species have unique features which allow them to produce silk through special glands. Using the website research these useful insects and describe how the silk-making process works. Find answers to the following.

1. What order of insects do silkworms belong to? _____

Draw pictures of the silkworm larva and cocoon in the boxes below:

2. Provide information on these aspects of the 'natural history' of the silk worm:

Food: _____

_____

Habitat: _____

_____

Interesting behaviors: _____

_____

3. The silk industry has a very old history. Use the website to provide some information on the points below. What can you deduce about the future of the silk industry?

The industry's history: _____

_____

_____

The industry today: _____

_____

_____

What I think about the future of the industry (and why): _____

_____

_____

First go to www.readyed.com.au/urls/critters

Beneficial Insects: Who's No. 1?

(Website: Click on Curious Critters: Beneficial Insects, Page 34, Site 1.)

❑ While we often think of insects such as flies and cockroaches as being pests, a great many insects are, in fact, beneficial to people. Use the website to make a list of your top five insects according to the information provided. Give reasons for your selections. Draw three of them.

Top of my list is . . . *(drum roll, please)*

_____

because_____

_____

_____

_____

_____

Picture 1

No. 3 on my list is . . .

_____

because_____

_____

_____

_____

_____

No. 2 on my list is . . .

_____

because_____

_____

_____

_____

No. 4 on my list is . . .

_____

because_____

_____

_____

_____

_____

Picture 2

Picture 3

No. 5 on my list is . . .

_____

because_____

_____

_____

_____

Curious Critters: Insects & Spiders, © 2004 Zephyr Press, Chicago, IL • 800-232-2187 • www.zephyrpress.com

Name: _____

Use the CD-ROM with this page.

Spiders: What is a Spider?—1
(Go to the Alternet CD-ROM section: Spiders—What is a Spider?)

❑ Spiders are part of the 71,000-strong arachnid family, which includes mites, ticks, scorpions and daddy-longlegs. Use the CD-ROM to note down some key points about spiders. Use the headings below.

1. Legs: _____

_____

2. Wings: _____

_____

3. Body parts: _____

_____

4. Eyes: _____

_____

5. Jaws: _____

_____

6. Other: _____

_____

_____

Diet
Describe how spiders catch and feed on their prey. _____

_____

What do spiders eat? _____

Common Spiders
What are the two groups of common spiders and how do they differ?

_____

_____

Choose a spider from each group and give a brief description of it. Include some information on its habitat.

_____

_____

_____

_____

_____

❊ ❊ **Level 2 Activities**

Spiders: What is a Spider?—2

(Go to the Alternet CD-ROM section: Spiders—What is a Spider?)

Spiders live everywhere in the world and come in all sizes, shapes and colors. They are often confused with insects but they are very different in lots of ways. Explore the CD-ROM to find out how.

Characteristics of Insects and Spiders

1. Use the information on the CD and complete the following table to demonstrate how spiders differ from insects.

Feature	Spider	Insects

2. Draw pictures of an insect and a spider in the boxes. Use the following labels in showing the differences between the two types of animals: 8 legs, 6 legs, wings, antennae, two-part body, three-part body, simple eyes, compound eyes, pedipalps, chelicerae .

Curious Critters: Insects & Spiders, © 2004 Zephyr Press, Chicago, IL • 800-232-2187 • www.zephyrpress.com

First go to www.readyed.com.au/urls/critters

✳ ✳ ✳ **Level 3 Activities**

Spiders: Humans and Spiders
(Website: Click on Curious Critters: Spiders, Page 37, Site 1.)

❑ Spiders are often feared by human beings, maybe because of the way they look, or perhaps because of fears about how poisonous they are. Some people are even terrified at the sight of a spider—a condition known as arachnophobia. But do spiders deserve this fearsome reputation? Look at your previous activity pages and **Website 1** to mount a 'for' and 'against' case on the subject of fear of spiders. Complete the table below by providing evidence to support each side of the argument.

Subject: Spiders Deserve to Be Feared by Humans.

The 'For' case:

_____
_____
_____
_____
_____

The 'Against' case:

_____
_____
_____
_____
_____

Your decision—Do spiders deserve their reputation?

_____
_____

Extra: Do an Internet search on movies or TV programs that are based on the fear of spiders, or that depict spiders as excessively dangerous creatures. What movies or programs can you find?

Name: _____

Use the CD-ROM with this page.

✳ **Level 1 Activities**

Spiders: The Tarantula—1
(Go to the Alternet CD-ROM section: Spiders—Tarantula)

❑ Tarantulas are amongst the most well known and feared spiders in the world but their bite is no more dangerous than any other spider. Use the Alternet CD-ROM to find out more about the world's largest spider.

Classification

1. What is the feature common to all tarantulas?
   How does a tarantula use this special feature to defend itself?

   _____

   _____

Habitat and Location

2. What conditions do tarantulas prefer? _____

   _____

   _____

3. Describe some of the ways a female tarantula will try to adapt her environment. _____

   _____

   _____

4. Describe the following body parts of a tarantula:

   carapace _____

   cephalothorax _____

   fangs _____

   pedipalp _____

   spinnerets _____

Diet

5. What do tarantulas eat and what is their diet dependent on? _____

   _____

   _____

Life Cycle

6. During a tarantula's life cycle they molt several times. What does this mean? _____

   _____

   _____

7. Why do female tarantulas live longer than male tarantulas? _____

   _____

   _____

Curious Critters: Insects & Spiders, © 2004 Zephyr Press, Chicago, IL • 800-232-2187 • www.zephyrpress.com

Name: _____

✳ ✳ **Level 2 Activities**

Spiders: The Tarantula—2
(Go to the Alternet CD-ROM section: Spiders—Tarantula)

❏ Tarantulas are normally quite long-living creatures who don't reach maturity for 10 years or so. In some cases females may live as long as 25 years, if they manage to avoid predators such as lizards and birds. Use the CD-ROM to track the life cycle of the tarantula. In each box write some key points about each stage of the cycle.

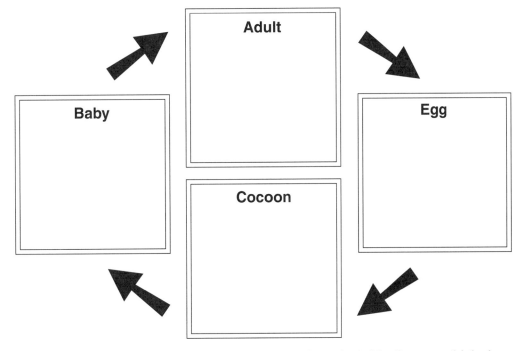

❏ Refer to the CD-ROM and the diagram of the tarantula. Complete this diagram which shows the various body parts of the spider. Make sure you label each part.

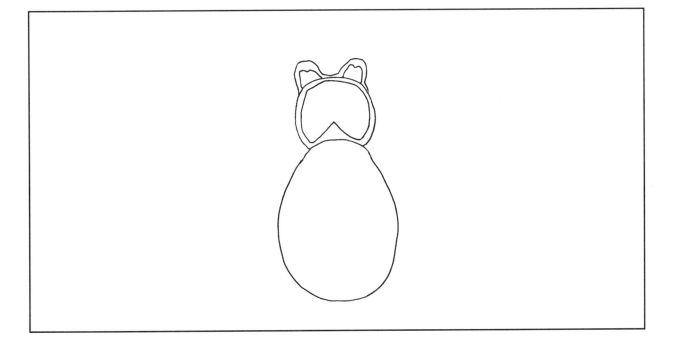

Curious Critters: Insects & Spiders, © 2004 Zephyr Press, Chicago, IL • 800-232-2187 • www.zephyrpress.com

❋ / ❋ ❋ **Level 1/2 Activities**

Spiders: Mites and Ticks

(Go to the Alternet CD-ROM section: Spiders—Mites and Ticks)

❑ Mites and ticks are related to spiders and scorpions and are among the oldest land animals, dating back 400 million years! Explore the CD-ROM to learn more about these diverse creatures.

Habitat

1. List some of the many habitats in which ticks and mites can survive. _____

_____

Description

2. Give a general description of the body of a mite. _____

_____

_____

3. How do ticks and mites use their pedipalps? _____

_____

4. How would you remove a wood tick? _____

_____

Life Cycle

5. What are the three stages of the life cycle? Give a brief description of each stage.

■ _____

_____

■ _____

_____

■ _____

_____

6. What does 'parasitic' mean? _____

_____

_____

Diseases

7. What different diseases can be caused by mites and ticks? Choose one disease and give a brief description of symptoms.

_____

_____

_____

Curious Critters: Insects & Spiders, © 2004 Zephyr Press, Chicago, IL • 800-232-2187 • www.zephyrpress.com

❋ ❋ ❋ **Level 3 Activities**

Spiders: Creative-Thinking Task Sheet

❑ An increased understanding of the skills shown below will help to develop your ability to think more creatively. What to do: Apply the skill to the Insects theme by following the instructions. Work on a large sheet of paper to end up with a chain of ideas, something like this:

Fluency The idea here is to come up with as many ideas as possible in the set time.	List all the types of spiders you can think of in a 2-minute time period.
Flexibility Try to provide as big a variety of ideas as you can.	Compare a spider with an insect. List the ways they are: • alike • different
Originality Provide new or unique solutions; perhaps put two known ideas together to form a third.	Think of unusual uses for spider webs. How you could market these commercially?
Elaboration Add on to what you already know to make an idea more exciting.	Substitute your body with a spider's body. How would life be different for you? What would be easier? What would be harder?
Curiosity Seek answers to questions by using Who? What? How? Why?	Why do you think spiders have segmented legs? Find out.
Complexity Look for different alternatives to what is provided or what you already know.	What questions can be asked to find out why spiders weave webs? Decide on the reasons why spiders are feared by humans.
Risk taking Accepting that there may be more than one correct answer but if you are mistaken that it doesn't equal failure.	Justify the tarantula's reputation.
Imagination Think beyond what is usually accepted as correct or true.	Think of a spider whose web has just been broken down for the 'umpteenth' time this week by a human running through it. How do you feel? What will you do? What do you think of humans?

Name: _____

Spiders: Spiders in Literature

❑ The spider has often featured in works of literature, in both poetry and prose. Below are some titles of poems and books in which spiders play a major role. Research each literary work and evaluate how the spider is depicted in the work. Is the spider the villain or the hero, or is it too difficult to decide? Write a brief summary of the work and make your judgement in the space provided.

1. *Little Miss Muffet* (traditional nursery rhyme)

   Summary _____
   _____
   _____

   Spider's role _____

2. *Itsy, Bitsy, Spider* (children's nursery rhyme and action song)

   Summary _____
   _____
   _____

   Spider's role _____

3. *The Redback on the Toilet Seat* (Australian poem by Slim Newton)

   Summary _____
   _____
   _____

   Spider's role _____

4. *Charlotte's Web* (children's book by E. B. White)

   Summary _____
   _____
   _____

   Spider's role _____

5. *The Very Busy Spider* (children's book by Eric Carle)

   Summary _____
   _____
   _____

   Spider's Role _____

APPENDICES: CONTENTS OF ALTERNET CD-ROM

What Is an Insect?

An insect is any living thing with three pairs of legs and a segmented body. This body is divided into three regions: the head; thorax; and abdomen. All insects are also characterized by their hard shell-like outer covering known as an exoskeleton.

There are many different types of insects. Some of the more common varieties include bees, ants, wasps, butterflies, cockroaches, ladybugs, fireflies, grasshoppers, crickets and beetles. There are so many different species of insect that if you were to list every single species you would need at least 6,000 sheets of paper! There are at least four times as many insects as the number of all the other animals combined.

The animal kingdom is thought to contain over 1.5 million different species. Of these, approximately one million are insects and an amazing 7,000–10,000 new insect species are discovered every year. The study of insects is known as entomology and entomologists believe that there are about one million to ten million insect species that have not yet been discovered.

Insects live almost everywhere on the earth, yet there are only a few species of insects that can live in the oceans. The range of insect species includes some of the most beautiful creatures on earth.

Their Bodies

All insects are characterized by their segmented body. Interestingly, the skeleton of an insect is on the outside of the body and is called the exoskeleton. An insect's head is made up of five or six pieces all joined together and includes the mouthparts, eyes and antennae. Insects and birds are the only animals that have wings. Nearly all adult insects have them, with insects such as mosquitoes and houseflies having two wings while butterflies, moths, dragonflies and wasps have four wings.

The Insect Life Cycle

Every insect starts life as an egg. After hatching, the insect begins to grow and develop. During this process, insects go through some dramatic changes to allow them to metamorphose into the adult stage. There are four stages of an insect's life:

egg   larva   pupa   adult

Humans and Insects

Many insects are considered pests by humans. These insects annoy us by biting and infecting us with deadly diseases. In addition, they attack valuable crops and can destroy pets and domestic animals by spreading their harmful diseases. They invade homes and eat food and can even destroy an entire house by eating the wood or building material.

However, there are some ways in which insects are helpful. They help to pollinate many of the crops by carrying seeds and provide us with unique products such as honey and silk. They are also a valuable food source for some of the animals that we eat such as fish and birds. We would probably not be able to live without insects as they play an important part in the animal food cycle.

Insect Life

Insects first appeared on earth about 400 million years ago. Over these millions of years they have evolved into an amazing range of different body forms and ways of life, adapting to a variety of different living conditions.

Strangely enough, insects do many of the same things we humans do. Some of them form colonies and build bridges and houses. Some insects raise crops and others keep cattle which they "milk". Some insects are carpenters, slaves, hunters and thieves and insects are even known to go to war to protect their territory.

Is a Spider an Insect?

Spiders, mites and ticks are often thought of as insects but they are really quite different. All insects have six legs while spiders have eight. A spider's body is divided into only two parts, unlike the insect with its three parts. Most insects have wings and antennae and these features are not found on any spider species.

Classification of Insects

All living things are categorized in the same way so that scientists all over the world are able to discuss the different species of animal or plant knowing that they are talking about the exact same species.

The sequence of classification involves the following headings.

Kingdom—This is the largest unit of classification and there are four kingdoms:

- **Animal**   - **Virus**
- **Plant**   - **Bacteria**

It was not until the development of the microscope that the virus and bacteria kingdoms were classified. Some biologists have classified living things into five kingdoms and on many occasions they disagree about what belongs in which group.

Phylum—Each kingdom can be divided into a number of phyla which are sometimes known as divisions. For example, there are about 30 phyla in the animal kingdom with insects and spiders being included in the phylum Arthropoda and human beings included in the phylum Chordata.

Class—Phyla are then divided into classes. Phylum Arthropoda includes insects, spiders, lobsters and related animals. Organisms that belong in the same class have more things in common with other members of this group. For example, animals that belong to the class Mammalia have hair on their bodies and feed milk to the their young while all animals that belong to the class Reptilia have scales that cover their bodies and are cold-blooded.

Order—There are thought to be about 30 orders in the class Insecta and these further classify different insects. It is often difficult for entomologists to agree on the exact number of orders in this class. Most names of orders end in one of these endings: *ura*—meaning tail; *ptera*—meaning wings; and *aptera* meaning wingless.

Family—This term classifies groups that are much more alike than orders.

Genus—Each living thing belongs to a genus and a species and these make up their 'scientific name.' Members of a genus are usually very similar but unable to breed with one another unless they are the same species.

Species—This is the basic unit of classification. Members of a species all have common characteristics and differ from all other living things in one way or another. This name is usually written in italics or is underlined. No two species in a genus have the same name and most of these names come from Greek or Latin words. All organisms are known by different common names around the world, however, their scientific name is always the same no matter what language.

The table below shows how three different animals are classified using this system.

	Human Beings	**Madagascar Hissing Cockroach**	**Orangutan**
Kingdom	Animalia	Animalia	Animalia
Phylum	Chordata	Arthropoda	Chordata
Class	Mammalia	Insecta	Mammalia
Order	Primate	Blattodea	Primate
Family	Hominidae	Blattidae	Hominidae
Genus	Homo	Grophadorhina	Pongo
Species	sapiens	portentosa	pygmaeus

Curious Critters: Insects & Spiders, © 2004 Zephyr Press, Chicago, IL • 800-232-2187 • www.zephyrpress.com

Classification of Insects *(cont.)*

Insects

The study of insects is known as entomology and scientists who study the classification of insects are known as entomologists. The class Insecta belongs to the bigger group Arthropoda which contains over 95% of the total animal species. All insects have the following three characteristics:

- A body divided into three parts covered with a hard exoskeleton
- Three pairs of legs
- A pair of antennae
- Many adult insects also have wings.

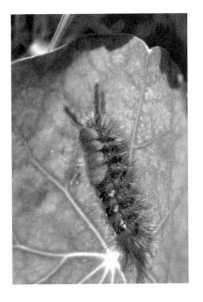

Here is a list of some of the orders of the class *Insecta* with the common name of the insect.

Scientific name	Common name
Apterygota	Wingless insects
Thysanura	Bristletails
Pterygota	Winged insects
Odonata	Dragonflies, damselflies
Ephemeroptera	Mayflies
Blattodea (Blattaria)	Cockroaches
Isopters	Termites
Mantodea	Praying mantis
Dermaptera	Earwigs
Plecoptera	Stoneflies
Orthoptera	Crickets, grasshoppers, locusts
Phasmatodea	Stick insects
Embioptera	Webspinners
Psocoptera	Booklice
Phtiraptera	Lice
Hemiptera	True bugs
Thysaoptera	Thrips, thunderflies
Megaloptera	Alderflies
Neuroptera	Ant lions, lacewings
Coleoptera	Beetles
Strepsiptera	Stylops
Mecoptera	Scorpionflies
Siphonaptera	Fleas
Diptera	Two-winged flies
Trichoptera	Caddisflies
Lepidoptera	Butterflies and moths
Hymenoptera	Sawflies, wasps, ants and bees
Zoraptera	Angel wings
Grylloblattodea (Grylloblattaria)	Rock crawlers
Archaeognatha (Microcoryphia)	Bristletails

Although this naming system is recognised all over the world, there is some confusion over the naming of certain groups, particularly insect orders. For example some entomologists include Homoptera in the order Hemiptera while others classify it as a separate order altogether. Usually, the Insecta class is known to contain 30 orders.

Features of Butterflies and Moths

Butterflies are among the most beautiful of insects with their vivid colors and amazing patterns. Their beauty is often featured in fairy tales, poems and art work around the world.

Moths are closely related to butterflies and together form the insect group Lepidoptera. The name Lepidoptera comes from two Greek words: *lepis*, meaning 'scale'; and *pteron*, meaning 'wing.' The name refers to the fine, powdery scales that cover the wings of butterflies and moths.

Moths are different from butterflies in a number of ways. Most butterflies fly during the day while moths prefer to fly at dusk or at night. The hind wing of moths is always attached to the front wing by a set of hooks and butterflies do not have this feature.

Also, the antennae of butterflies widen at the end and resemble clubs while moths are quite different. Butterflies tend to be much more colorful than moths and some female moths do not even have wings.

They have many body features in common with other insects such as the hard exoskeleton and the three main parts of the body; the head, thorax and abdomen.

The anatomy of butterflies and moths changes through their different life stages.

The Caterpillar

Caterpillars are usually a solid green or brown color, with only a few of them having patterns or bright colors. Their skin can vary from being very smooth to having bristly hair and bumps.

Their bodies are made up of 14 segments. The first segment contains the head which includes the mouthparts, and two short antennae. The head has tiny eyes on each side and although they cannot see images, they are able to distinguish between light and dark.

The next three segments make up the thorax, with each segment having two legs and a little claw attached. The rest of the segments make up the abdomen and often contain what are described as false legs, which have a tiny hook at the end.

The last segment has two sucker-like legs which allow the caterpillar to cling to plants.

Another feature is the short spinneret which sticks out of the caterpillar's mouth, releasing a sticky liquid that turns into a silken thread.

The caterpillar stage lasts for at least two weeks and in this time the exoskeleton does not grow at all. It splits along the back when it is too tight for the body. The way in which a caterpillar sheds its exoskeleton is fascinating. Once the old one is shed, it must lie very still to wait for the new one to harden, but first the caterpillar stretches the soft skeleton a little bit to allow for more growing room. This process is probably done four or five times before a caterpillar reaches the pupa stage in the life cycle.

The New Adult

When a butterfly reaches the adult stage of the life cycle, many interesting things occur. Its body gives off a fluid that allows it to break out of the shell it was in. The thorax then swells and cracks the shell and then both the head and thorax emerge.

The exoskeleton is soft and the wings are damp and crumpled. Special muscles allow the butterfly to pump air and blood into its body and wings. After a short while the exoskeleton hardens and other body parts get ready. The proboscis (nose part which helps the insect suck up nectar from plants) is split in half and the butterfly uses its front legs to join the proboscis together. After only an hour, the butterfly is ready for take-off.

Sadly, butterflies have a very short life span. Some only live for two weeks, yet other species are known to live for as long as 18 months.

Common Insects—Types of Beetles

Beetles are one of the most common types of insects and there are at least 300,000 different species which live everywhere except the oceans.

Amazingly, beetles are able to exist in areas as extreme as deserts, mountain lakes, tropical rainforests, and even polluted drains.

Like most other insects beetles have three pairs of legs, a tough exoskeleton, a head, thorax, abdomen and antennae. What makes them different from other insects is their pair of front wings called *elytra*. These form leathery covers that protect the beetle's body.

They have a shell-like body and hard wing covers which makes them quite different in appearance to the other members of the insect world.

Most species of beetles are solitary insects. They make up the insect order Coleoptera which comes from a Greek word meaning "sheath wings". It refers to the beetle's elytra, which form a sheath (cover) for much of the upper body. The order Coleoptera is the largest order of insects and nearly 40% of insect species belong to it. This order is divided into about 150 families. Some of the main families of beetles include:

Weevils (Curculionidae)

Leaf beetles (Chrysomelidae)

Ground beetles (Carabidae)

Ladybugs (Ladybirds) (Coccinellidae)

Fireflies (Lampyridae)

Rove beetles (Staphylinidae)

Scarabs (Scarabaeidae)

Click beetles (Elateridae)

Predacious diving beetles (Dytiscidae)

Common Insects—Fearless Flies

A fly is an insect with one pair of wings which belongs to the order Diptera in the Insecta class. There are around 100,000 different species of flies with the common house fly probably the best known.

Other varieties of fly include blow flies, black flies, bot flies, crane flies, deer flies, mosquitoes, sand flies, robber flies, tsetse flies and fruit flies.

A number of other insects such as dragonflies and mayflies are often called flies but are not true flies as they usually have four wings rather than two.

Flies, like most insects, have a life cycle divided into four stages; the egg stage, larvae, pupa and adult. The average life span only lasts 30 days with flies living longer in cooler weather.

Pests

Some flies are considered to be dangerous pests responsible for carrying germs and disease that can greatly affect animals and plants. The germs are carried inside their bodies, on the tips of their mouthparts or in hair on their bodies. When a fly bites or touches something it usually leaves some of those germs behind.

Flies can transmit diseases such as malaria, sleeping sickness, dysentery and filariasis.

Some kinds of flies are helpful and carry pollen from one plant to another like bees. Other flies eat smaller insects. The fruit fly is particularly useful to scientists studying heredity.

Controlling Flies

Scientists have developed many ways to control the spread of flies even though we still seem to have flies always around us. Some of the ways include draining swamps or covering them with oil and insecticides. These treatments kill newly hatched mosquitoes and other flies that grow in water.

Types of Flies

Fruit fly—This fly produces larvae which eat their way through a variety of fruits, making them one of the most harmful agricultural pests. Members of one family of these insects are called peacock flies because of their habit of strutting on fruit. They are small insects with many colors and beautiful wings. They lay their eggs in fruits, berries, nuts and other parts of plants. Larvae that hatch from the eggs are small white maggots that tunnel their way through the fruit. This family of fruit flies includes the destructive Mediterranean fruit fly, Oriental fruit fly, Mexican fruit fly, the various cherry fruit flies and the apple maggot.

There are efforts made to control the growth of these flies which include applying chemical sprays and introducing the flies' natural enemies. Another control technique involves releasing large numbers of sterilized male flies. A female fly that mates with one of the sterilized males cannot produce fertile eggs.

Mosquitoes—There are more than 3,000 species of mosquitoes and these insects spread some of the worst diseases of people and animals. Certain kinds of mosquitoes carry the germs that cause such serious diseases as encephalitis and yellow fever. When a mosquito "bites", it may leave germs behind. Many kinds of mosquitoes do not spread diseases but they have painful bites that can turn into welts on sensitive skin. Many of the mosquitoes that are associated with disease live in the hot, moist lands near the equator, although mosquitoes are found in all parts of the world, even in the Arctic.

Sand Flies—These are hairy, dark brown insects that measure about .13 inches (3.2 millimeters) long. Female sand flies are active at night and suck blood from human beings and animals. Their larvae live in moist places and feed on decaying plant and animal matter.

Most types of sand flies live and thrive in the tropics and subtropics. They transmit germs that cause such serious diseases as kala-azar and sand fly fever.

Moth flies are related to sand flies, but they do not suck blood. Their wings fold over their bodies like a roof. Biting midges are sometimes called sand flies. In spring and autumn biting midges may appear in swarms. They rank among the smallest blood-sucking insects and some are only .04 inches (1 millimeter) long.

Sand flies, moth flies, and biting midges are all in the true fly order, Diptera.

Common Insects—Fearless Flies *(cont.)*

Tsetse Fly—This is a two-winged fly of Africa which carries the animal parasites that cause African sleeping sickness. There are about 20 kinds of tsetse flies and most of them attack people. The flies look like ordinary houseflies but they are larger and fold their wings flat over their backs in such a way that the wings do not stick out at an angle as they do on houseflies. The tsetse fly has a long proboscis (beak) that it uses to pierce the skin of its victim. It sucks the blood of mammals and as it sucks the blood, it infects its victim.

The tsetse fly can transmit deadly diseases to animals and people. The flies usually cannot infect people or animals until the germs have lived in their bodies several days and have passed through the stomach to their salivary glands. Then, for at least 96 days, the flies can transmit the parasites to anyone they bite.

Tsetse flies breed slowly. The female fly produces only one egg at a time. The larva hatches from the egg and is nourished during the growing period inside the body of the parent. When the larva is fully grown, it is deposited on the ground and becomes a pupa.

Both male and female flies are active bloodsuckers. They are found chiefly along lake edges and riverbanks, making parts of Africa uninhabitable. In some regions, insecticide sprays control tsetse fly populations. Other control programs use radiation to sterilize male flies, making them unable to reproduce. Drugs that protect cattle from sleeping sickness are also used.

Social Insects—The Honeybee Colony

Three main insect orders are considered to be social insects; the Hymenoptera - which include ants, bees and wasps; the Isoptera which include termites and the Homoptera which include aphids.

Some species of bees and ants are known as *social insects*. This is because they live in organized communities called colonies. All species of termites and certain wasps are also known as social insects.

Other types of bees prefer to live alone and are classified as **solitary bees.**

Social Bees

The way in which these bee colonies function is very interesting. In some ways they are very similar to the ways in which humans exist. Honeybees appear to have the most highly developed societies. Read below to find out how these complex colonies function.

The Colony

The honeybee colony is made up of one queen bee, tens of thousands of worker bees and a few hundred drones. The worker bees and the drones are all offspring of the queen. The worker bees are all female and the drones are all male.

The Hive

All honeybees live in a hive which is basically a storage box containing a honeycomb. The honeycomb is made up of many cells joined together. These cells are hexagon shaped and are made from wax that the worker bees produce. The cells containing the eggs and developing bees are known as the brood nests and are in the middle of the hive. The bees store pollen and honey around this nest.

Bees have to protect their hive and its contents from other animals, including other bee colonies. There are always several worker bees guarding the entrance. Interestingly, the bees in each hive have their own special smell and these guard bees can detect the smell of other bees and will attack.

Bees will attack any animal with their stinger and when the threat of danger is great, such as a bear or human being coming near the hive, the guard bees produce a special scent which alerts the other bees in the hive to come and help the guards.

Finding Food

Flowers are the main source of food and provide bees with pollen and nectar. Pollen is an important source of fats, proteins, vitamins and minerals which are necessary for the developing bee. The sugar in the nectar is the main source of energy.

Scout bees search for food for the hive and perform a type of dance to show the rest of the bees where the food is in relation to the sun. A similar dance is done by the scout bees when they search for a new location for a hive.

Making Honey

Flowers have special glands called nectaries which produce nectar. Worker honeybees suck up nectar from the flowers with their tongues and store it in their honey stomachs. When a worker has filled up its stomach with a load of nectar, it returns to the hive and spits out the nectar. It usually gives the nectar to other bees or puts it in an empty cell in the hive. Worker bees add certain enzymes (special chemicals) and then the water evaporates, changing the nectar to honey.

Social Insects—The Honeybee Colony *(cont.)*

Making Wax

Special wax-producing glands develop in the abdomen of the workers when they are about ten days old. The workers eat large amounts of honey and these glands then convert the honey to wax. This wax then leaks out through the small holes in the bee's body and forms tiny white flakes on the outside of the abdomen. The bee then picks off the flakes and moves them up to its jaws. It chews the wax and then adds it to the honeycomb that it is building. The only time bees produce beeswax is when they need wax to build the honeycomb.

Swarming

When a colony becomes overcrowded, the queen stops laying eggs for a while. The workers build cells for the new queens and the old queen deposits the eggs into these cells. In a few days, after the new queen cells are covered over with wax, many of the workers and the old queen leave the hive as a swarm. Their flight to form a new colony is called swarming. The swarm usually gathers around a branch or post after leaving the hive. Then scout bees go in search of a new location for the hive and use a special dance to direct other scouts to the site to check it out as a new location. At a given signal, the entire swarm travels to whichever site is chosen as the best. Streaker bees lead the way and the queen bee follows.

Enemies

Bees have many enemies that want to get to the hive. Bears, ants, humans and other animals may destroy the hive while skunks and dragonflies may eat the bees. A species of moth, the wax moth, is known to eat the wax in the honeycomb and the worker bees have to try and protect their colony by stinging any intruders but this does not always work.

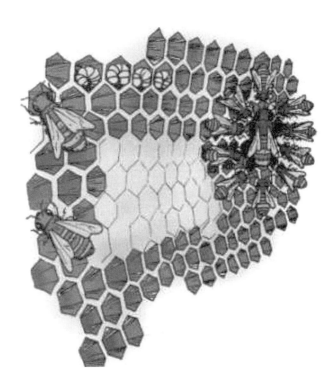

Beneficial Insects—The Praying Mantis

Praying mantids (mantis) are a fascinating group of insects that exist throughout the tropics and sunny areas in southern Europe, North America, Canada and South America. There are about 2,000 named species of mantids.

The praying mantis gets it name from the Greek word for 'prophet.' This is because the mantis has a habit of standing still for a long time with its forelegs held folded up before it, making it look similar to someone praying. It is also referred to as the *preying* mantis because it preys on other insects and small creatures.

Classification

Praying mantids belong to the suborder Mantodea which is one of the orders of the class Insecta. There is some confusion about which suborder Mantodea belong to as some entomologists have placed them in the Dictyoptera order with cockroaches and some have placed them in the Orthoptera order with crickets and grasshoppers.

Physical Appearance

A fully grown adult mantid can measure up to 5 inches (13 centimeters) long depending on the species. The largest species is found in Sri Lanka and can reach a length of almost 10 inches (25 centimeters), feeding on birds and small reptiles as well as other insects.

Mantids are able to camouflage themselves to hide from predators. Many mantids are colored and adorned with outgrowths that enable them to look like grass, leaves, flowers and pieces of stick. A species of mantid known as the Malaysian Orchid mantid can look just like the flower in its early stages of life but it loses this unique ability once it becomes an adult mantid.

Most species are winged though females rarely fly after mating as they are too heavy with eggs. Mantids tend to fly more at night which brings them to the attention of bats who are a main predator of mantids. They usually have two pairs of wings which fold neatly against the abdomen when not being used. The back wings are mainly used for flying and startling enemies.

Characteristics

All mantids have a triangular head with large compound eyes, two antennae and a collection of sharp mouth parts designed for eating prey. They have excellent eyesight, however, the sharpest vision is located in the center and so they must rotate their heads and look directly at an object. The mantis is able to rotate its head 180 degrees to see prey or approaching enemies. Their eyes change color from light green or tan in bright light, to dark brown in the dark.

The prothorax or neck helps them locate and capture prey as it is quite flexible. This prothorax helps identify mantids among other insects.

Life Cycle

Mantids reproduce in much the same way as all other insects and then metamorphose into the adult stage. They do not however, have a larval stage. Instead they go through several stages all of which look like miniature wingless adults. This whole process is known as *incomplete metamorphosis*. Males and females are easy to tell apart as there are six abdominal segments in the females and eight segments in the male.

Beneficial Insects—The Praying Mantis *(cont.)*

Interesting Habits

Mantids are carnivorous and are known to prey on many other insects and are even capable of eating small tree frogs. They only eat live prey or prey that is moving and males are thought to be less aggressive than the females. A mantid uses its arm-like forelegs to grasp and capture its prey. The forelegs have sharp spines and hooks that dig into the victim.

Baby mantids often eat other baby mantids and adult mantids will even eat their own babies as well as other babies if they cannot find other insects to prey on. They usually eat during the day and are known to gather around artificial light sources.

A female mantid will sometimes eat the male mantid that she is mating with. In some species this is a necessary process as it allows the male to release the sperm for the eggs. Strangely enough, the male is still able to continue mating even after its head and brain have been eaten! When the male eventually dies he is used as a source of protein for the female and her young.

The female can lay her eggs the day after mating in a process which can take between three and five hours.

Defense

A mantid has four ways of defending itself from enemies:

- **Camouflage**

- **Standing Still**—The praying mantis is able to stand still for many hours at a time causing it to be overlooked by predators.

- **Startle-Display**—When confronted by an enemy the mantid can rear up on its hind legs and spread and rattle its wings to scare off other insects.

- **Ultrasonic Ear**—Mantids, unlike any other animals, have only one ear which is made of a deep .04 inch (1 millimeter) long slit with cuticle-like knobs at either end and two ear drums buried inside. It is especially tuned to high frequencies and responds to echolocation signals that are sent out by bats, their main enemy.

Spiders: What Is a Spider?

Classification

The spider belongs to the arachnid family which includes mites, ticks, scorpions and daddy-longlegs. There are 71,000 different species of arachnids. Spiders live everywhere in the world and come in all sizes, colors and shapes. The smallest spider is about the size of a pinhead and the largest measures almost 10 inches (25 centimeters) across from one side of its body to the other.

Characteristics of a Spider

Although insects and spiders are often confused there are many differences between them. The most obvious is that spiders have eight walking legs and insects have six. Most insects have wings and antennae while spiders do not. A spider's body is divided into two parts, the cephalothorax and abdomen (stomach area). These two parts are joined by a narrow waist. In comparison an insect's body is divided into three parts.

Spiders have simple eyes and usually they have eight of them while an insect has two big compound eyes.

Spiders do not have the same type of jaws as insects do. Beneath the front end of the cephalothorax are the spider's two-segmented weapons called chelicerae.

Additionally, spiders have leg-like appendages called pedipalps or "palps" at each side of their mouth that aid in manipulating and breaking the body of the prey.

Diet

All spiders are predators, feeding mainly on insects and all spiders have venom. Spiders cover their victim's body with strong digestive juices that dissolve the internal organs of their prey. The liquid is then sucked into the mouth by the spider's powerful stomach muscles.

Web Spinning

All spiders have glands within their abdomens that dispense silk through tube-like spinning organs called spinnerets and all species of spiders spin cocoons to protect their developing young. Many spiders spin webs as snares to capture insects.

Types of Common Spiders

Spiders can be divided into one of two groups depending on how they capture their prey. One group is the hunting spider and the other is the web-building spider. Although all spiders produce silk they do not all use the silk to construct webs. Hunting or wandering spiders do not construct webs to capture food. Instead, they rely on their quickness and relatively good eyesight to capture their prey.

Web-building spiders construct webs in rather quiet, undisturbed places to capture their food. They live in or near their webs and wait for food to come to them. They generally have poor eyesight and rely on sensing vibrations in their webs to detect prey.

Some common hunting spiders are the jumping spiders, wolf spiders, fishing spiders, sac spiders, crab spiders and gnaphosid spiders.

Some common web-building spiders are the comb-footed spider, the orb spider and the grass spider.

Curious Critters: Insects & Spiders, © 2004 Zephyr Press, Chicago, IL • 800-232-2187 • www.zephyrpress.com

Spiders: The Tarantula

Classification

Different species of tarantulas occur in many parts of the world, the largest being a tropical spider found in South America. Tarantula is the common name of any one of a group of mostly large, hairy spiders. They get their name from the wolf spider that is common in Taranto, Italy. Its body may look fierce, but its bite is usually no more dangerous than other spiders.

However, the body hairs of a tarantula may induce an allergic reaction. Some tarantulas may live for more than 20 years.

Habitat and Location

Tarantulas are commonly found in warm climates and the tropics. They prefer to live in dry, well-drained soil. If the soil is suitable, the female digs a deep burrow which she lines with silk webbing. This helps prevent sand and dirt from trickling in. Otherwise, she hides in cracks in logs and under any loose-lying debris. In winter, she covers the entrance to her home with a plug of leaves and silk, and lies dormant in her den until the return of spring. She also uses the burrow as a safe retreat for molting, and for guarding her cocoon and the newly hatched young.

Description

Tarantulas are all quite fearsome in appearance with their long, hairy legs and body covered with an almost mouse-like fur.

Diet

The tarantula's diet consists of both invertebrates and small vertebrates. Some tarantulas will even eat small birds. In Brazil, tarantulas have been known to eat reptiles and amphibians. The diet of this spider varies according to where they live.

Behavior

The tarantula does not spin a web to capture its prey, but catches food by quickly seizing its prey and killing it with venom. Through the wound made by the fangs, the tarantula injects an enzyme from its mouth which makes the prey easier to digest. This fluid or enzyme reduces the prey to a consistency where it may be sucked in by the spider with the aid of its strong stomach muscles. It is then absorbed in the tarantula's stomach.

Life Cycle

Tarantulas are normally long-lived creatures. They do not reach maturity for about ten years. During this time they undergo a series of molts, and until they reach maturity you can't tell the male from the female. The mature male is quite dark, nearly black, while the mature female is brown.

After mating, the male lives only a short time. It may die a natural death or be eaten by the female, sometimes even before mating can occur. When it comes time for egg laying, the female spins a large sheet of webbing on which she deposits numerous large pearly white eggs. They are covered by a second sheet of webbing which is tightly bound at the edges. She guards this flattened egg sac or cocoon carefully for six or seven weeks until the eggs are hatched.

Baby tarantulas stay in the mother's burrow for a week or so before they leave and establish dens of their own. Some females may live as long as 25 years, but long life in the wild is rare for they have many enemies such as lizards, snakes and spider-eating birds.

The Tarantula's Bite

Even if, through carelessness, a bite should occur, the venom when injected into humans causes only slight swelling, with some numbness and itching which disappears in a short time.

Spiders: Mites and Ticks

Classification

Mites and ticks are small animals related to spiders and scorpions. They are the most diverse of all arachnids. Mites belong to the order Acarina and are amongst the oldest land animals, with fossils identified as being 400 million years old.

Habitat

Mites are found throughout the world, living in environments ranging from freezing cold conditions to deserts to rainforests. Some mites live on land, while others live in sea water, ponds or lakes. They seem to be able to survive in almost any environment. Some water mites crawl on stones and others swim. Of the land mites and ticks, some live on people, on dogs, on cheese, in birds' noses and feathers, in monkeys' lungs, on other bugs and insect eggs, on bat wings, and in bees' throats. Others live on plants and crops, in soil and leaf litter and decaying wood.

Description

Some mites are too small to be seen without the use of a microscope and most mites are less than .04 inches (1 millimeter) long. Ticks can be larger with a wood tick growing up to .12 inches (3 centimeters) long. The adult usually has a sac-like body with a slight dividing line between its abdomen and thorax, and has four pairs of legs. The mouth has piercing and grasping organs. These organs are used to sink their mouth into the flesh of their host and feed on their blood.

Some mites can tuck their legs under hinged "wings" forming a little ball. Many have plates on the back and underside. Some worm-like microscope gall mites have fewer legs. Mites have a simple claw on their pedipalps or none at all.

Life Cycle

Ticks and mites have three distinct life stages. The young larvae of most species hatch from eggs and have six legs. After a meal of blood from the host, they shed their skins and change into nymphs with eight legs. After one or more other moltings, the nymphs change into an adult.

Life Style

Many kinds of mites and ticks live at least part of their lives as parasites. They suck the blood of animals or the juice from plants. Other mites eat feathers, cheese, flour, cereal, drugs, and other stored products. Several kinds of mites burrow into the skin of people and other mammals, especially horses, cattle, and sheep. They cause the skin to break out and itch, forming scabs (this condition is called scabies) and mange.

Diseases Caused by Mites and Ticks

Lyme Disease—Lyme disease is a bacterial infection that is transmitted by the deer tick and causes symptoms ranging from a rash, fever, and headaches to painful swelling in the joints. The disease can be treated successfully but if it is not treated early enough, it can cause permanent damage to the heart and nervous system.

Rocky Mountain Spotted Fever—Rocky Mountain spotted fever is an infectious disease carried by rodents. It is transmitted by infected ticks that attach themselves to humans. Symptoms include chills, high fever and a severe rash which can spread over the whole body.

Varroa and Honeybees—Varroa mites are external honeybee parasites that attack both the adults and the brood, with a distinct preference for drone blood. They suck the blood from both the adults and the developing brood, weakening and shortening the life span of the ones on which they feed. The emerging brood may be deformed with missing legs or wings. Untreated infestations of varroa mites that are allowed to increase will kill honeybee colonies.

Spiders: Mites and Ticks *(cont.)*

Dust Mites—There are many species of dust mites as well as predatory mites that share the same dusty environment. Dust mites live in the fine layer of minute dust particles that continually settles on household items. They are found almost world wide but their numbers are considerably reduced at high altitudes and dry climates. House dust mites have been known to be associated with allergies for a long time. They do not bite or sting but harbor strong allergens in their bodies as well as in their secretions, excreta and the skin that they shed. Constant contact with these allergens can cause breathing and skin problems in humans.

Scabies—Scabies mites burrow into a person's skin and cause severe itching all over the body, especially at night. Large areas of the body can be covered by a rash that can last for weeks but which will not (or only rarely) coincide with the areas of mite infestation. Scabies mites tend to burrow into the skin where there is a natural crease like hands, and webbing between the fingers, the wrists and elbows.

Answers

Page 8: Finding Out About Insects—1

1. " any living thing with three pairs of legs and a segmented body."
2. head, thorax, abdomen—descriptions will vary.
3. Definitions as from CD.

Page 9: Finding Out About Insects—2

1. Answers will vary
2. a. Metamorphosis is the word used by biologists to describe how an insect develops from an egg into an adult.
2. b. Answers will vary.

Page 10: Classification of Insects—1

2. Table

	Humans	**Cockroach**	**Orangutan**
Kingdom	Animalia	Animalia	Animalia
Phylum	Chordata	Arthropoda	Chordata
Class	Mammalia	Insecta	Mammalia
Order	Primate	Blattodea	Primate
Family	Hominidae	Blattidae	Hominidae
Genus	Homo	Grophadorhina	Pongo
species	sapiens	portentosa	pygmaeus

Page 11: Classification of Insects—2

Questions: 1. Kingdom; 2. species; 3. *Homo sapiens;* 4. *Grophadorhina portentosa;* 5. Animal or Animalia;
6. Arthropoda or Arthropods; 7. Class insecta; 8. About 30, some say 32; 9. ptera—meaning wings, ura—meaning tail and aptera—meaning wingless. 10. jointed feet; 11. cockroaches, beetles, bees, butterflies, etc.
Common names: Lice; butterflies and moths; beetles; stick insects; termites; praying mantis.

Pages 12, 13

Answers will vary.

Page 14: Insects Puzzle

Across: 3. delicate; 4. venom; 6. camouflage; 11. thorax; 12. colony; 14. bee; 16. carnivorous; 19. exoskeleton; 23. antennae; 24. nocturnal

Down: 1. six; 2. segments; 5. emerge; 7. appearance; 8. larva; 9. species; 10. vibration; 13. nymph; 15. molt; 16. caterpillar; 17. nectar; 18. compound; 20. drones; 21. defend; 22. cavity.

Pages 15–20

Answers will vary.

Page 21: Butterflies and Moths—1

1. a. eyes, antennae, palpi and proboscis
1. b. 11 parts; reproductive organs and organs for digesting food.
1. c. 3 parts; legs and wings.
2. Answers will vary.

Page 22: Butterflies and Moths—2

1. 14; 2. the first; 3. spinneret; 4. 2 weeks; 5. front legs; 6. about an hour; 7. cocoon; 8. 2 weeks to 18 months.

Page 23

Answers will vary.

Page 24: The Honeybee

Three types of bees are worker bees, queens and drones.
Other answers will vary.

Curious Critters: Insects & Spiders, © 2004 Zephyr Press, Chicago, IL • 800-232-2187 • www.zephyrpress.com

Pages 25–30

Answers will vary.

Page 31: Beneficial Insects—Praying Mantis 1

Habitat: Tropics and sunny areas in southern Europe, North America, Canada and South America.
Classification: prophet; Mantodea; Insecta; preying.
Rest of answers will vary.

Pages 32–34

Answers will vary.

Page 35: What is a Spider?—1

Diet: Spiders cover their victim's body with strong digestive juices that dissolve the internal organs of their prey. The liquid is then sucked into the mouth by the spider's powerful stomach muscles.
Eat mainly insects
Two groups of spiders are: hunting spider; web-building spider.

Pages 36–37

Answers will vary.

Page 38: The Tarantula—1

1. Hairy bodies; Hairs can induce an allergic reaction; 2. Dry, well-drained soil; 3. Digs a burrow, covers entrance to burrow, lines burrow with silk; 4. Answer will vary. 5. Invertebrates, vertebrates, birds, reptiles, amphibians. Varies depending where spider lives. 6. They shed their exoskeleton. 7. The female eats the male.

Page 39

Answers will vary.

Page 40: Mites and Ticks

1. Land, water, hot, cold, on animals and plants; 2. Answers will vary; 3. Leg-like organs used for catching prey; 4. Answers will vary; 5. Egg, larvae, nymph; 6. Living off a host; 7. Lyme, Rocky Mountain Spotted Fever, varroa, mange, scabies.

Curious Kids Love *Curious Critters!*

Curious Critters of the Natural World
MAMMALS

Curious Critters of the Natural World
REPTILES & AMPHIBIANS

Mammals that lay eggs? *4,000* species of ladybugs? Your students will clamor to use the *Curious Critters* CD and workbooks as they learn cool facts about the world's living creatures.

Each title includes CD "Alternet" (works with both Windows and Macintosh operating systems) and 64-page book. Internet browser required for some activities.

Curious Critters of the Natural World
Mammals
Grades 4–7
ISBN: 1-56976-159-0
1112-W . . . $24.95

Curious Critters of the Natural World
Reptiles & Amphibians
Grades 4–7
ISBN: 1-56976-160-4
1113-W . . . $24.95

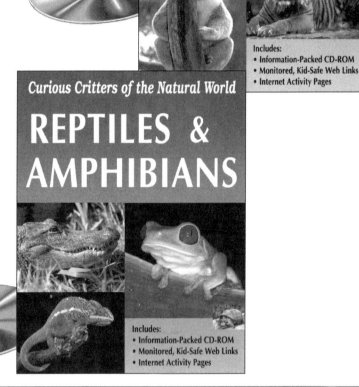

THE SCIENCE OF LIFE
Projects and Principles for Beginning Biologists

Frank G. Bottone, Jr.

A Smithsonian Notable Book for Children

"At once a lively introduction to the scientific method and a survey of hands-on-experiemnts, this outstanding overview touches on important concepts in botany, bacteriology, molecular biology, mycology, microbiology, and more."—*Smithsonian*

Grades 4 and up
144 pages, paper
ISBN: 1-55652-382-3
LIFE-W . . . $14.95 (CAN$22.95)